Alfred Tennyson

The Death of Oenone, Akbar's Dream, and Other Poems

Alfred Tennyson

The Death of Oenone, Akbar's Dream, and Other Poems

ISBN/EAN: 9783337006068

Printed in Europe, USA, Canada, Australia, Japan

Cover: Foto ©Thomas Meinert / pixelio.de

More available books at **www.hansebooks.com**

THE
DEATH OF ŒNONE,
AKBAR'S DREAM,
AND OTHER POEMS

BY

ALFRED
LORD TENNYSON

POET LAUREATE

𝔏𝔬𝔫𝔡𝔬𝔫

MACMILLAN AND CO.

AND NEW YORK

1892

CONTENTS

CONTENTS

JUNE BRACKEN AND HEATHER

To ——

THERE on the top of the down,

The wild heather round me and over me June's
high blue,

When I look'd at the bracken so bright and the
heather so brown,

I thought to myself I would offer this book to
you,

This, and my love together,

To you that are seventy-seven,

Œ   B

With a faith as clear as the heights of the June-

blue heaven,

And a fancy as summer-new

As the green of the bracken amid the gloom of

the heather.

TO THE MASTER OF BALLIOL

I

DEAR Master in our classic town,

You, loved by all the younger gown

There at Balliol,

Lay your Plato for one minute down,

II

And read a Grecian tale re-told,

Which, cast in later Grecian mould,

Quintus Calaber

Somewhat lazily handled of old;

III

And on this white midwinter day—

For have the far-off hymns of May,

All her melodies,

All her harmonies echo'd away?—

IV

To-day, before you turn again

To thoughts that lift the soul of men,

Hear my cataract's

Downward thunder in hollow and glen,

V

Till, led by dream and vague desire,

The woman, gliding toward the pyre,

Find her warrior

Stark and dark in his funeral fire.

THE DEATH OF ŒNONE

THE DEATH OF ŒNONE

ŒNONE sat within the cave from out

Whose ivy-matted mouth she used to gaze

Down at the Troad; but the goodly view

Was now one blank, and all the serpent vines

Which on the touch of heavenly feet had risen,

And gliding thro' the branches overbower'd

The naked Three, were wither'd long ago,

And thro' the sunless winter morning-mist

In silence wept upon the flowerless earth.

 And while she stared at those dead cords that

  ran

Dark thro' the mist, and linking tree to tree,

But once were gayer than a dawning sky

With many a pendent bell and fragrant star,

Her Past became her Present, and she saw

Him, climbing toward her with the golden fruit,

Him, happy to be chosen Judge of Gods,

Her husband in the flush of youth and dawn,

Paris, himself as beauteous as a God.

Anon from out the long ravine below,

She heard a wailing cry, that seem'd at first

Thin as the batlike shrillings of the Dead

When driven to Hades, but, in coming near,

Across the downward thunder of the brook

Sounded 'Œnone'; and on a sudden he,

Paris, no longer beauteous as a God,

Struck by a poison'd arrow in the fight,

Lame, crooked, reeling, livid, thro' the mist

Rose, like the wraith of his dead self, and moan'd

' Œnone, *my* Œnone, while we dwelt

Together in this valley—happy then—

Too happy had I died within thine arms,

Before the feud of Gods had marr'd our peace,

And sunder'd each from each.   I am dying now

Pierced by a poison'd dart.   Save me.   Thou

    knowest,

Taught by some God, whatever herb or balm

May clear the blood from poison, and thy fame

Is blown thro' all the Troad, and to thee

The shepherd brings his adder-bitten lamb,

The wounded warrior climbs from Troy to thee.

My life and death are in thy hand.   The Gods

Avenge on stony hearts a fruitless prayer

For pity.   Let me owe my life to thee.

I wrought thee bitter wrong, but thou forgive,

Forget it.   Man is but the slave of Fate.

Œnone, by thy love which once was mine,

Help, heal me.   I am poison'd to the heart.'

'And I to mine' she said 'Adulterer,

Go back to thine adulteress and die!'

He groan'd, he turn'd, and in the mist at once

Became a shadow, sank and disappear'd,

But, ere the mountain rolls into the plain,

Fell headlong dead; and of the shepherds one

Their oldest, and the same who first had found

Paris, a naked babe, among the woods

Of Ida, following lighted on him there,

And shouted, and the shepherds heard and came.

One raised the Prince, one sleek'd the squalid

    hair,

One kiss'd his hand, another closed his eyes,

And then, remembering the gay playmate rear'd

Among them, and forgetful of the man,

Whose crime had half unpeopled Ilion, these

All that day long labour'd, hewing the pines,

And built their shepherd-prince a funeral pile ;

And, while the star of eve was drawing light

From the dead sun, kindled the pyre, and all

Stood round it, hush'd, or calling on his name.

But when the white fog vanish'd like a ghost

Before the day, and every topmost pine

Spired into bluest heaven, still in her cave,

Amazed, and ever seeming stared upon

By ghastlier than the Gorgon head, a face,—

His face deform'd by lurid blotch and blain—

There, like a creature frozen to the heart

Beyond all hope of warmth, Œnone sat

Not moving, till in front of that ravine

Which drowsed in gloom, self-darken'd from the west,

The sunset blazed along the wall of Troy.

    Then her head sank, she slept, and thro' her
      dream
A ghostly murmur floated, 'Come to me,
Œnone! I can wrong thee now no more,
Œnone, my Œnone,' and the dream
Wail'd in her, when she woke beneath the stars.

    What star could burn so low? not Ilion yet.
What light was there? She rose and slowly down,
By the long torrent's ever-deepen'd roar,
Paced, following, as in trance, the silent cry.
She waked a bird of prey that scream'd and past;
She roused a snake that hissing writhed away;
A panther sprang across her path, she heard
The shriek of some lost life among the pines,
But when she gain'd the broader vale, and saw
The ring of faces redden'd by the flames

Enfolding that dark body which had lain

Of old in her embrace, paused—and then ask'd

Falteringly, 'Who lies on yonder pyre?'

But every man was mute for reverence.

Then moving quickly forward till the heat

Smote on her brow, she lifted up a voice

Of shrill command, 'Who burns upon the pyre?'

Whereon their oldest and their boldest said,

'He, whom thou wouldst not heal!' and all at
   once

The morning light of happy marriage broke

Thro' all the clouded years of widowhood,

And muffling up her comely head, and crying

'Husband!' she leapt upon the funeral pile,

And mixt herself with *him* and past in fire.

ST. TELEMACHUS

ST. TELEMACHUS

HAD the fierce ashes of some fiery peak

Been hurl'd so high they ranged about the globe?

For day by day, thro' many a blood-red eve,

In that four-hundredth summer after Christ,

The wrathful sunset glared against a cross

Rear'd on the tumbled ruins of an old fane

No longer sacred to the Sun, and flamed

On one huge slope beyond, where in his cave

The man, whose pious hand had built the cross,

A man who never changed a word with men,

Fasted and pray'd, Telemachus the Saint.

c

Eve after eve that haggard anchorite

Would haunt the desolated fane, and there

Gaze at the ruin, often mutter low

'Vicisti Galilæe'; louder again,

Spurning a shatter'd fragment of the God,

'Vicisti Galilæe!' but—when now

Bathed in that lurid crimson—ask'd 'Is earth

On fire to the West? or is the Demon-god

Wroth at his fall?' and heard an answer 'Wake

Thou deedless dreamer, lazying out a life

Of self-suppression, not of selfless love.'

And once a flight of shadowy fighters crost

The disk, and once, he thought, a shape with
        wings

Came sweeping by him, and pointed to the West,

And at his ear he heard a whisper 'Rome'

And in his heart he cried 'The call of God!'

And call'd arose, and, slowly plunging down

Thro' that disastrous glory, set his face

By waste and field and town of alien tongue,

Following a hundred sunsets, and the sphere

Of westward-wheeling stars ; and every dawn

Struck from him his own shadow on to Rome.

   Foot-sore, way-worn, at length he touch'd his goal,

The Christian city. All her splendour fail'd

To lure those eyes that only yearn'd to see,

Fleeting betwixt her column'd palace-walls,

The shape with wings. Anon there past a crowd

With shameless laughter, Pagan oath, and jest,

Hard Romans brawling of their monstrous games ;

He, all but deaf thro' age and weariness,

And muttering to himself ' The call of God '

And borne along by that full stream of men,

Like some old wreck on some indrawing sea,

Gain'd their huge Colosseum.　The caged beast

Yell'd, as he yell'd of yore for Christian blood.

Three slaves were trailing a dead lion away,

One, a dead man.　He stumbled in, and sat

Blinded ; but when the momentary gloom,

Made by the noonday blaze without, had left

His aged eyes, he raised them, and beheld

A blood-red awning waver overhead,

The dust send up a steam of human blood,

The gladiators moving toward their fight,

And eighty thousand Christian faces watch

Man　murder　man.　A　sudden　strength　from

　　heaven,

As some great shock may wake a palsied limb,

Turn'd him again to boy, for up he sprang,

And glided lightly down the stairs, and o'er

The barrier that divided beast from man

Slipt, and ran on, and flung himself between

The gladiatorial swords, and call'd ' Forbear

In the great name of Him who died for men,

Christ Jesus ! ' For one moment afterward

A silence follow'd as of death, and then

A hiss as from a wilderness of snakes,

Then one deep roar as of a breaking sea,

And then a shower of stones that stoned him

dead,

And then once more a silence as of death.

His dream became a deed that woke the world,

For while the frantic rabble in half-amaze

Stared at him dead, thro' all the nobler hearts

In that vast Oval ran a shudder of shame.

The Baths, the Forum gabbled of his death,

And preachers linger'd o'er his dying words,

Which would not die, but echo'd on to reach

Honorius, till he heard them, and decreed

That Rome no more should wallow in this old lust

Of Paganism, and make her festal hour

Dark with the blood of man who murder'd man.

(For Honorius, who succeeded to the sovereignty over
Europe, supprest the gladiatorial combats practised of old
in Rome, on occasion of the following event.   There was
one Telemachus, embracing the ascetic mode of life, who
setting out from the East and arriving at Rome for this
very purpose, while that accursed spectacle was being per-
formed, entered himself the circus, and descending into the
arena, attempted to hold back those who wielded deadly
weapons against each other.   The spectators of the murderous fray, possest with the drunken glee of the demon who
delights in such bloodshed, stoned to death the preacher of
peace.   The admirable Emperor learning this put a stop to
that evil exhibition.—Theodoret's *Ecclesiastical History.*)

AKBAR'S DREAM

AKBAR'S DREAM

O GOD in every temple I see people that see thee, and in every language I hear spoken, people praise thee.

Polytheism and Islám feel after thee.

Each religion says, ' Thou art one, without equal.'

If it be a mosque people murmur the holy prayer, and if it be a Christian Church, people ring the bell from love to Thee.

Sometimes I frequent the Christian cloister, and sometimes the mosque.

But it is thou whom I search from temple to temple.

Thy elect have no dealings with either heresy or orthodoxy; for neither of them stands behind the screen of thy truth.

Heresy to the heretic, and religion to the orthodox,

But the dust of the rose-petal belongs to the heart
of the perfume seller.

AKBAR *and* ABUL FAZL *before the palace at*
Futehpur-Sikri at night.

'LIGHT of the nations' ask'd his Chronicler

Of Akbar 'what has darken'd thee to-night?'

Then, after one quick glance upon the stars,

And turning slowly toward him, Akbar said

'The shadow of a dream—an idle one

It may be.   Still I raised my heart to heaven,

I pray'd against the dream.   To pray, to do—

To pray, to do according to the prayer,

Are, both, to worship Alla, but the prayers,

That have no successor in deed, are faint

And pale in Alla's eyes, fair mothers they

Dying in childbirth of dead sons.   I vow'd

Whate'er my dreams, I still would do the right

Thro' all the vast dominion which a sword,

That only conquers men to conquer peace,

Has won me.   Alla be my guide !

                                            But come,

My noble friend, my faithful counsellor,

Sit by my side.   While thou art one with me,

I seem no longer like a lonely man

In the king's garden, gathering here and there

From each fair plant the blossom choicest-grown

To wreathe a crown not only for the king

But in due time for every Mussulmân,

Brahmin, and Buddhist, Christian, and Parsee,

Thro' all the warring world of Hindustan.

   Well spake thy brother in his hymn to heaven

" Thy glory baffles wisdom.   All the tracks

Of science making toward Thy Perfectness

Are blinding desert sand ; we scarce can spell

The Alif of Thine alphabet of Love."

He knows Himself, men nor themselves nor
    Him,
For every splinter'd fraction of a sect
Will clamour "*I* am on the Perfect Way,
All else is to perdition."

                Shall the rose
Cry to the lotus "No flower thou"? the palm
Call to the cypress "I alone am fair"?
The mango spurn the melon at his foot?
"Mine is the one fruit Alla made for man."

Look how the living pulse of Alla beats
Thro' all His world.   If every single star
Should shriek its claim "I only am in heaven"
Why that were such sphere-music as the Greek
Had hardly dream'd of.   There is light in all,
And light, with more or less of shade, in all

Man-modes of worship; but our Ulama,

Who "sitting on green sofas contemplate

The torment of the damn'd" already, these

Are like wild brutes new-caged—the narrower

The cage, the more their fury.   Me they front

With sullen brows.   What wonder!   I decreed

That even the dog was clean, that men may taste

Swine-flesh, drink wine; they know too that when-

    e'er

In our free Hall, where each philosophy

And mood of faith may hold its own, they blurt

Their furious formalisms, I but hear

The clash of tides that meet in narrow seas,—

Not the Great Voice not the true Deep.

                          To drive

A people from their ancient fold of Faith,

And wall them up perforce in mine—unwise,

Unkinglike ;—and the morning of my reign

Was redden'd by that cloud of shame when I . . .

    I hate the rancour of their castes and creeds,

I let men worship as they will, I reap

No revenue from the field of unbelief.

I cull from every faith and race the best

And bravest soul for counsellor and friend.

I loathe the very name of infidel.

I stagger at the Korân and the sword.

I shudder at the Christian and the stake ;

Yet " Alla," says their sacred book, " is Love,"

And when the Goan Padre quoting Him,

Issa Ben Mariam, his own prophet, cried

" Love one another little ones " and " bless "

Whom? even "your persecutors"! there methought

The cloud was rifted by a purer gleam

Than glances from the sun of our Islâm.

And thou rememberest what a fury shook

Those pillars of a moulder'd faith, when he,

That other, prophet of their fall, proclaimed

His Master as "the Sun of Righteousness,"

Yea, Alla here on earth, who caught and held

His people by the bridle-rein of Truth.

What art thou saying? "And was not Alla call'd

In old Irân the Sun of Love? and Love

The net of truth?"

A voice from old Irân!

Nay, but I know it—*his*, the hoary Sheik,

On whom the women shrieking "Atheist" flung

Filth from the roof, the mystic melodist

Who all but lost himself in Alla, him

Abû Saîd——

—a sun but dimly seen

Here, till the mortal morning mists of earth

Fade in the noon of heaven, when creed and race

Shall bear false witness, each of each, no more,

But find their limits by that larger light,

And overstep them, moving easily

Thro' after-ages in the love of Truth,

The truth of Love.

                    The sun, the sun ! they rail

At me the Zoroastrian.   Let the Sun,

Who heats our earth to yield us grain and fruit,

And laughs upon thy field as well as mine,

And warms the blood of Shiah and Sunnee,

Symbol the Eternal !   Yea and may not kings

Express Him also by their warmth of love

For all they rule—by equal law for all?

By deeds a light to men?

                    But no such light

Glanced from our Presence on the face of one,

Who breaking in upon us yestermorn,

With all the Hells a-glare in either eye,

Yell'd "hast *thou* brought us down a new Korân

From heaven? art *thou* the Prophet? canst *thou* work

Miracles?" and the wild horse, anger, plunged

To fling me, and fail'd.   Miracles! no, not I

Nor he, nor any.   I can but lift the torch

Of Reason in the dusky cave of Life,

And gaze on this great miracle, the World,

Adoring That who made, and makes, and is,

And is not, what I gaze on—all else Form,

Ritual, varying with the tribes of men.

 Ay but, my friend, thou knowest I hold that forms

Are needful: only let the hand that rules,

With politic care, with utter gentleness,

Mould them for all his people.

And what are forms?

Fair garments, plain or rich, and fitting close

Or flying looselier, warm'd but by the heart

Within them, moved but by the living limb,

And cast aside, when old, for newer,—Forms!

The Spiritual in Nature's market-place—

The silent Alphabet-of-heaven-in-man

Made vocal—banners blazoning a Power

That is not seen and rules from far away—

A silken cord let down from Paradise,

When fine Philosophies would fail, to draw

The crowd from wallowing in the mire of earth,

And all the more, when these behold their Lord,

Who shaped the forms, obey them, and himself

Here on this bank in *some* way live the life

Beyond the bridge, and serve that Infinite

Within us, as without, that All-in-all,

And over all, the never-changing One

And ever-changing Many, in praise of Whom

The Christian bell, the cry from off the mosque,

And vaguer voices of Polytheism

Make but one music, harmonising " Pray."

  There westward—under yon slow-falling star,

The Christians own a Spiritual Head ;

And following thy true counsel, by thine aid,

Myself am such in our Islâm, for no

Mirage of glory, but for power to fuse

My myriads into union under one ;

To hunt the tiger of oppression out

From office ; and to spread the Divine Faith

Like calming oil on all their stormy creeds,

And fill the hollows between wave and wave ;

To nurse my children on the milk of Truth,

And alchemise old hates into the gold

Of Love, and make it current; and beat back

The menacing poison of intolerant priests,

Those cobras ever setting up their hoods—

One Alla! one Kalifa!

                    Still—at times

A doubt, a fear,—and yester afternoon

I dream'd,—thou knowest how deep a well of

    love

My heart is for my son, Saleem, mine heir,—

And yet so wild and wayward that my dream—

He glares askance at thee as one of those

Who mix the wines of heresy in the cup

Of counsel—so—I pray thee——

                    Well, I dream'd

That stone by stone I rear'd a sacred fane,

A temple, neither Pagod, Mosque, nor Church,

But loftier, simpler, always open-door'd

To every breath from heaven, and Truth and Peace

And Love and Justice came and dwelt therein ;

But while we stood rejoicing, I and thou,

I heard a mocking laugh " the new Korân ! "

And on the sudden, and with a cry " Saleem "

Thou, thou—I saw thee fall before me, and then

Me too the black-wing'd Azrael overcame,

But Death had ears and eyes ; I watch'd my son,

And those that follow'd, loosen, stone from stone,

All my fair work ; and from the ruin arose

The shriek and curse of trampled millions, even

As in the time before ; but while I groan'd,

From out the sunset pour'd an alien race,

Who fitted stone to stone again, and Truth,

Peace, Love and Justice came and dwelt therein,

Nor in the field without were seen or heard

Fires of Súttee, nor wail of baby-wife,

Or Indian widow; and in sleep I said

" All praise to Alla by whatever hands

My mission be accomplish'd ! " but we hear

Music : our palace is awake, and morn

Has lifted the dark eyelash of the Night

From off the rosy cheek of waking Day.

Our hymn to the sun.   They sing it.   Let us go.'

HYMN

I

Once again thou flamest heavenward, once again
    we see thee rise.

Every morning is thy birthday gladdening human
    hearts and eyes.

Every morning here we greet it, bowing

lowly down before thee,

Thee the Godlike, thee the changeless in thine

ever-changing skies.

II

Shadow-maker, shadow-slayer, arrowing light from

clime to clime,

Hear thy myriad laureates hail thee monarch in

their woodland rhyme.

Warble bird, and open flower, and, men,

below the dome of azure

Kneel adoring Him the Timeless in the flame that

measures Time !

NOTES TO AKBAR'S DREAM

The great Mogul Emperor Akbar was born October 14, 1542, and died 1605. At 13 he succeeded his father Humayun; at 18 he himself assumed the sole charge of government. He subdued and ruled over fifteen large provinces; his empire included all India north of the Vindhya Mountains—in the south of India he was not so successful. His tolerance of religions and his abhorrence of religious persecution put our Tudors to shame. He invented a new eclectic religion by which he hoped to unite all creeds, castes and peoples : and his legislation was remarkable for vigour, justice and humanity.

' *Thy glory baffles wisdom.*' The Emperor quotes from a hymn to the Deity by Faizi, brother of Abul Fazl, Akbar's chief friend and minister, who wrote the *Ain i Akbari* (Annals of Akbar). His influence on his age was immense. It may be that he and his brother Faizi led Akbar's mind

away from Islám and the Prophet—this charge is brought
against him by every Muhammadan writer; but Abul Fazl
also led his sovereign to a true appreciation of his duties,
and from the moment that he entered Court, the problem of
successfully ruling over mixed races, which Islám in few
other countries had to solve, was carefully considered, and
the policy of toleration was the result (Blochmann xxix.).

Abul Fazl thus gives an account of himself 'The advice
of my Father with difficulty kept me back from acts of folly;
my mind had no rest and my heart felt itself drawn to the
sages of Mongolia or to the hermits on Lebanon. I longed
for interviews with the Llamás of Tibet or with the padres
of Portugal, and I would gladly sit with the priests of the
Parsis and the learned of the Zendavesta. I was sick of the
learned of my own land.'

He became the intimate friend and adviser of Akbar,
and helped him in his tolerant system of government.
Professor Blochmann writes 'Impressed with a favourable
idea of the value of his Hindu subjects, he (Akbar) had
resolved when pensively sitting in the evenings on the
solitary stone at Futehpur-Sikri to rule with an even hand
all men in his dominions; but as the extreme views of the
learned and the lawyers continually urged him to perse-
cute instead of to heal, he instituted discussions, because,
believing himself to be in error, he thought it his duty as
ruler to inquire.' 'These discussions took place every
Thursday night in the Ibadat-khana a building at Futehpur-
Sikri, erected for the purpose' (Malleson).

In these discussions Abul Fazl ·became a great power, and he induced the chief of the disputants to draw up a document defining the 'divine Faith' as it was called, and assigning to Akbar the rank of a Mujahid, or supreme khalifah, the vicegerent of the one true God.

Abul Fazl was finally murdered at the instigation of Akbar's son Salim, who in his Memoirs declares that it was Abul Fazl who had perverted his father's mind so that he denied the divine mission of Mahomet, and turned away his love from his son.

Faizi. When Akbar conquered the North-West Provinces of India, Faizi, then 20, began his life as a poet, and earned his living as a physician. He is reported to have been very generous and to have treated the poor for nothing. His fame reached Akbar's ears who commanded him to come to the camp at Chitor. Akbar was delighted with his varied knowledge and scholarship and made the poet teacher to his sons. Faizi at 33 was appointed Chief Poet (1588). He collected a fine library of 4300 MSS. and died at the age of 40 (1595) when Akbar incorporated his collection of rare books in the Imperial Library.

The warring world of Hindostan. Akbar's rapid conquests and the good government of his fifteen provinces with their complete military, civil and political systems make him conspicuous among the great kings of history.

The Goan Padre. Abul Fazl relates that 'one night

the Ibadat-khana was brightened by the presence of Padre Rodolpho, who for intelligence and wisdom was unrivalled among Christian doctors. Several carping and bigoted men attacked him and this afforded an opportunity for the display of the calm judgment and justice of the assembly. These men brought forward the old received assertions, and did not attempt to arrive at truth by reasoning. Their statements were torn to pieces, and they were nearly put to shame, when they began to attack the contradictions of the Gospel, but they could not prove their assertions. With perfect calmness, and earnest conviction of the truth he replied to their arguments.'

Abû Sa'îd. 'Love is the net of Truth, Love is the noose of God' is a quotation from the great Sufee poet Abû Sa'îd —born A.D. 968, died at the age of 83. He is a mystical poet, and some of his expressions have been compared to our George Herbert. Of Shaikh Abû Sa'îd it is recorded that he said, 'when my affairs had reacht a certain pitch I buried under the dust my books and opened a shop on my own account (*i.e.* began to teach with authority), and verily men represented me as that which I was not, until it came to this, that they went to the Qâdhî and testified against me of unbelieverhood; and women got upon the roofs and cast unclean things upon me.' (*Vide* reprint from article in *National Review*, March 1891, by C. J. Pickering.)

Aziz. I am not aware that there is any record of such

intrusion upon the king's privacy, but the expressions in the text occur in a letter sent by Akbar's foster-brother Aziz, who refused to come to court when summoned and threw up his government, and 'after writing an insolent and reproachful letter to Akbar in which he asked him if he had received a book from heaven, or if he could work miracles like Mahomet that he presumed to introduce a new religion, warned him that he was on the way to eternal perdition, and concluded with a prayer to God to bring him back into the path of salvation' (Elphinstone).

'The Koran, the Old and New Testament, and the Psalms of David are called *books* by way of excellence, and their followers "People of the Book"' (Elphinstone).

Akbar according to Abdel Kadir had his son Murad instructed in the Gospel, and used to make him begin his lessons 'In the name of Christ' instead of in the usual way 'In the name of God.'

> *To drive*
> *A people from their ancient fold of Truth,* etc.

Malleson says 'This must have happened because Akbar states it, but of the forced conversions I have found no record.   This must have taken place whilst he was still a minor, and whilst the chief authority was wielded by Bairam.'

> '*I reap no revenue from the field of unbelief*'

The Hindus are fond of pilgrimages and Akbar removed

a remunerative tax raised by his predecessors on pilgrimages. He also abolished the fezza or capitation tax on those who differed from the Mahomedan faith. He discouraged all *excessive* prayers, fasts and pilgrimages.

Suttee. Akbar decreed that every widow who showed the least desire not to be burnt on her husband's funeral pyre, should be let go free and unharmed.

baby-wife. He forbad marriage before the age of puberty.

Indian widow. Akbar ordained that remarriage was lawful.

Music. 'About a watch before daybreak,' says Abul Fazl, the musicians played to the king in the palace. 'His Majesty had such a knowledge of the science of music as trained musicians do not possess.'

'*The Divine Faith.*' The Divine Faith slowly passed away under the immediate successors of Akbar. An idea of what the Divine Faith was may be gathered from the inscription at the head of the poem. The document referred to, Abul Fazl says 'brought about excellent results (1) the Court became a gathering place of the sages and learned of all creeds ; the good doctrines of all religious systems were recognized, and their defects were not allowed to obscure their good features ; (2) perfect toleration or peace with all

was established ; and (3) the perverse and evil-minded were
covered with shame on seeing the disinterested motives of
His Majesty, and these stood in the pillory of disgrace.'
Dated September 1579—Ragab 987 (Blochmann xiv.).

THE BANDIT'S DEATH

TO SIR WALTER SCOTT [1]

O GREAT AND GALLANT SCOTT,
TRUE GENTLEMAN, HEART, BLOOD AND BONE,
I WOULD IT HAD BEEN MY LOT
TO HAVE SEEN THEE, AND HEARD THEE, AND KNOWN.

[1] I have adopted Sir Walter Scott's version of the following story as given in his last journal (Death of Il Bizarro)—but I have taken the liberty of making some slight alterations.

THE BANDIT'S DEATH

SIR, do you see this dagger? nay, why do you start

   aside?

I was not going to stab you, tho' I *am* the Bandit's

   bride.

You have set a price on his head : I may claim it

   without a lie.

What have I here in the cloth?   I will show it you

   by-and-by.

                              .

Sir, I was once a wife.   I had one brief summer

   of bliss.

                        E

But the Bandit had woo'd me in vain, and he
    stabb'd my Piero with this.

And he dragg'd me up there to his cave in the
    mountain, and there one day
He had left his dagger behind him.   I found it.
    I hid it away.

For he reek'd with the blood of Piero; his kisses
    were red with his crime,
And I cried to the Saints to avenge me.   They
    heard, they bided their time.

In a while I bore him a son, and he loved to
    dandle the child,   ·
And that was a link between us; but I—to be
    reconciled ?—

No, by the Mother of God, tho' I think I hated
   him less,
And—well, if I sinn'd last night, I will find the
   Priest and confess.

Listen ! we three were alone in the dell at the
   close of the day.
I was lilting a song to the babe, and it laugh'd like
   a dawn in May.

Then on a sudden we saw your soldiers crossing
   the ridge,
And he caught my little one from me : we dipt
   down under the bridge

By the great dead pine—you know it—and heard
   as we crouch'd below,

The clatter of arms, and voices, and men passing
to and fro.

Black was the night when we crept away—not a
star in the sky—
Hush'd as the heart of the grave, till the little one
utter'd a cry.

I whisper'd 'give it to me,' but he would not
answer me—then
He gript it so hard by the throat that the boy
never cried again.

We return'd to his cave—the link was broken—
he sobb'd and he wept,
And cursed himself; then he yawn'd, for the wretch
could sleep, and he slept

Ay, till dawn stole into the cave, and a ray red.
as blood

Glanced on the strangled face—I could make Sleep

Death, if I would—

Glared on at the murder'd son, and the murderous
father at rest, . . .

I drove the blade that had slain my husband thrice

thro' his breast.

He was loved at least by his dog : it was chain'd,
but its horrible yell

'She has kill'd him, has kill'd him, has kill'd him'

rang out all down thro' the dell,

Till I felt I could end myself too with the dagger

—so deafen'd and dazed—

Take it, and save me from it !   I fled.   I was all
    but crazed

With the grief that gnaw'd at my heart, and the
    weight that dragg'd at my hand ;
But thanks to the Blessed Saints that I came on
    none of his band ;

And the band will be scatter'd now their gallant
    captain is dead,
For I with this dagger of his—do you doubt me ?
    Here is his head !

THE CHURCH-WARDEN AND

THE CURATE

THE CHURCH-WARDEN AND THE CURATE

This is written in the dialect which was current in my youth at Spilsby and in the country about it.

I

Eh? good daäy! good daäy! thaw it bean't not
   mooch of a daäy,

Nasty, casselty weather! an' mea haäfe down wi'
   my haäy!

II

How be the farm gittin on? noäways.   Gittin on
    i'deeäd !

Why, tonups was haäfe on 'em fingers an' toäs, an'
    the mare brokken-kneeäd,

An' pigs didn't sell at fall, an' wa lost wer Hal-
    deny cow,

An' it beäts ma to knaw wot she died on, but wool's
    looking oop ony how.

III

An' soä they've maäde tha a parson, an' thou'll git
    along, niver fear,

Fur I beän chuch-warden mysen i' the parish fur
    fifteen year.

Well—sin ther beä chuch-wardens, ther mun be
parsons an' all,
An' if t'ōne stick alongside t'uther the chuch weänt
happen a fall.

IV

Fur I wur a Baptis wonst, an' ageän the toithe an'
the raäte,
Till I fun that it warn't not the gaäinist waäy to
the narra Gaäte.
An' I can't abeär 'em, I can't, fur a lot on 'em
coom'd ta-year—
I wur down wi' the rheumatis then—to *my* pond
to wesh thessens theere—
Sa I sticks like the ivin as long as I lives to the
owd chuch now,

Fur they wesh'd their sins i' *my* pond, an' I doubts

they poison'd the cow.

V

Ay, an' ya seed the Bishop.   They says 'at he

coom'd fra nowt—

Burn i' traäde.   Sa I warrants 'e niver said haafe

wot 'e thowt,

But 'e creeäpt an' 'e crawl'd along, till 'e feeäld 'e

could howd 'is oän,

Then 'e married a greät Yerl's darter, an' sits o'

the Bishop's throän.

VI

Now I'll gie tha a bit o' my mind an' tha weant

be taakin' offence,

Fur thou be a big scholard now wi' a hoonderd

haäcre o' sense—

But sich an obstropulous lad—naay, naay—fur I

minds tha sa well,

Tha'd niver not hopple thy tongue, an' the tongue's

sit afire o' Hell,

As I says to my missis to-daay, when she hurl'd a

plaäte at the cat

An' anoother ageän my noäse. Ya was niver sa

bad as that.

VII

But I minds when i' Howlaby beck won daäy ya

was ticklin' o' trout,

An' keeäper 'e seed ya an roon'd, an' 'e beal'd to

ya 'Lad coom hout'

An' ya stood oop naäkt i' the beck, an' ya tell'd
'im to knaw his awn plaäce
An' ya call'd 'im a clown, ya did, an' ya thraw'd the
fish i' 'is faäce,
An' 'e torn'd as red as a stag-tuckey's wattles, but
theer an' then
I coämb'd 'im down, fur I promised ya'd niver
not do it ageän.

VIII

An' I cotch'd tha wonst i' my garden, when thou
was a height-year-howd,
An' I fun thy pockets as full o' my pippins as iver
they'd 'owd,
An' thou was as peärky as owt, an' tha maäde me
as mad as mad,

But I says to tha 'keeap 'em, an' welcome' fur thou
was the Parson's lad.

IX

An' Parson 'e 'ears on it all, an' then taäkes kindly
to me,
An' then I wur chose Chuch-warden an' coom'd
to the top o' the tree,
Fur Quoloty's hall my friends, an' they maäkes ma
a help to the poor,
When I gits the plaäte fuller o' Soondays nor ony
chuch-warden afoor,
Fur if iver thy feyther 'ed riled me I kep' mysen
meeäk as a lamb,
An' saw by the Graäce o' the Lord, Mr. Harry, I
ham wot I ham.

X

But Parson 'e *will* speäk out, saw, now 'e be sixty-
seven,

He'll niver swap Owlby an' Scratby fur owt but
the Kingdom o' Heaven ;

An' thou'll be 'is Curate 'ere, but, if iver tha meäns
to git 'igher,

Tha mun tackle the sins o' the Wo'ld, an' not the
faults o' the Squire.

An' I reckons tha'll light of a livin' somewheers i'
the Wowd or the Fen,

If tha cottons down to thy betters, an' keeäps thysen to thysen.

But niver not speäk plaain out, if tha wants to git
forrards a bit,

But creeäp along the hedge-bottoms, an' thou'll be
a Bishop yit.

XI

Naäy, but tha *mun* speäk hout to the Baptises here

    i' the town,

Fur moäst on 'em talks ageän tithe, an' I'd like

    tha to preäch 'em down,

Fur *they*'ve bin a-preächin' *mea* down, they heve,

    an' I haätes 'em now,

Fur they leäved their nasty sins i' *my* pond, an' it

    poison'd the cow.

F

'Casselty,' casualty, chance weather.

'Haäfe down wi' my haäy,' while my grass is only half-mown.

'Fingers and toes,' a disease in turnips.

'Fall,' autumn.

'If t'ōne stick alongside t'uther,' if the one hold by the other. One is pronounced like 'own.'

'Fun,' found.

'Gaäinist,' nearest.

'Ta-year,' this year.

'Ivin,' ivy.

'Obstropulous,' obstreperous—here the Curate makes a sign of deprecation.

'Hopple' or 'hobble,' to tie the legs of a skittish cow when she is being milked.

'Beal'd,' bellowed.

In such words as 'torned' (turned), 'hurled,' the *r* is hardly audible.

'Stag-tuckey,' turkey-cock.

'Height-year-howd,' eight-year-old.

''Owd,' hold.

'Pearky,' pert.

'Wo'ld,' the world. Short *o*.

'Wowd,' wold.

CHARITY

CHARITY

I

WHAT am I doing, you say to me, 'wasting the
sweet summer hours'?

Haven't you eyes? I am dressing the grave of a
woman with flowers.

II

For a woman ruin'd the world, as God's own
scriptures tell,

And a man ruin'd mine, but a woman, God bless
her, kept me from Hell.

III

Love me ?   O yes, no doubt—how long—till you

threw me aside !

Dresses and laces and jewels and never a ring for

the bride.

IV

All very well just now to be calling me darling and

sweet,

And after a while would it matter so much if I came

on the street ?

V

You when I met you first—when *he* brought you !

—I turn'd away

And the hard blue eyes have it still, that stare of a

beast of prey.

VI

You were his friend—you—you—when he pro-

mised to make me his bride,

And you knew that he meant to betray me—you

knew—you knew that he lied.

VII

He married an heiress, an orphan with half a shire

of estate,—

I sent him a desolate wail and a curse, when I

learn'd my fate.

VIII

For I used to play with the knife, creep down to

the river-shore,

Moan to myself 'one plunge—then quiet for ever-

more.'

IX

Would the man have a touch of remorse when he

heard what an end was mine?

Or brag to his fellow rakes of his conquest over

their wine?

X

Money—my hire—*his* money—I sent him back

what he gave,—

Will you move a little that way? your shadow

falls on the grave.

XI

Two trains clash'd : then and there he was crush'd

in a moment and died,

But the new-wedded wife was unharm'd, tho' sitting

close at his side.

XII

She found my letter upon him, my wail of reproach
and scorn;
I had cursed the woman he married, and him, and
the day I was born.

XIII

They put him aside for ever, and after a week—no
more—
A stranger as welcome as Satan—a widow came to
my door:

XIV

So I turn'd my face to the wall, I was mad, I was
raving-wild,
I was close on that hour of dishonour, the birth of
a baseborn child.

XV

O you that can flatter your victims, and juggle, and

lie and cajole,

Man, can you even guess at the love of a soul for

a soul?

XVI

I had cursed her as woman and wife, and in wife

and woman I found

The tenderest Christ-like creature that ever stept

on the ground.

XVII

She watch'd me, she nursed me, she fed me, she

sat day and night by my bed,

Till the joyless birthday came of a boy born happily

dead.

XVIII

And her name? what was it? I ask'd her. She

    said with a sudden glow

On her patient face ' My dear, I will tell you before

    I go.'

XIX.

And I when I learnt it at last, I shriek'd, I sprang

    from my seat,

I wept, and I kiss'd her hands, I flung myself

    down at her feet,

XX

And we pray'd together for *him*, for *him* who had

    given her the name.

She has left me enough to live on. I need no

    wages of shame.

XXI

She died of a fever caught when a nurse in a hos-

pital ward.

She is high in the Heaven of Heavens, she is face

to face with her Lord,

XXII

And He sees not her like anywhere in this pitiless

world of ours !

I have told you my tale.   Get you gone.   I am

dressing her grave with flowers.

KAPIOLANI

Kapiolani was a great chieftainess who lived in the
Sandwich Islands at the beginning of this century.
She won the cause of Christianity by openly defying
the priests of the terrible goddess Peelè. In spite of
their threats of vengeance she ascended the volcano
Mauna-Loa, then clambered down over a bank of
cinders 400 feet high to the great lake of fire (nine
miles round)—Kilauëä—the home and haunt of the
goddess, and flung into the boiling lava the conse-
crated berries which it was sacrilege for a woman to
handle.

I

WHEN from the terrors of Nature a people have

fashion'd and worship a Spirit of Evil,

Blest þe the Voice of the Teacher who calls to

them

' Set yourselves free ! '

II

Noble the Saxon who hurl'd at his Idol a valorous

weapon in olden England !

Great and greater, and greatest of women, island

heroine, Kapiolani

Clomb the mountain, and flung the berries, and

dared the Goddess, and freed the people

Of Hawa-i-ee !

III

A people believing that Peelè the Goddess would

wallow in fiery riot and revel

On Kilauēä,

Dance in a fountain of flame with her devils, or

shake with her thunders and shatter her

island,

Rolling her anger

Thro' blasted valley and flaring forest in blood-red

cataracts down to the sea !

IV

Long as the lava-light

Glares from the lava-lake

Dazing the starlight,

Long as the silvery vapour in daylight

Over the mountain

Floats, will the glory of Kapiolani be mingled with

either on Hawa-i-ee.

V

What said her Priesthood ?

'Woe to this island if ever a woman should handle

or gather the berries of Peelè !

Accursèd were she !

And woe to this island if ever a woman should

    climb to the dwelling of Peelè the Goddess !

Accurséd were she ! '

VI

One from the Sunrise

Dawn'd on His people, and slowly before him

Vanish'd shadow-like

Gods and Goddesses,

None but the terrible Peelè remaining as Kapio-

    lani ascended her mountain,

Baffled her priesthood,

Broke the Taboo,

Dipt to the crater,

Call'd on the Power adored by the Christian, and

    crying ' I dare her, let Peelè avenge herself ' !

Into the flame-billow dash'd the berries, and drove

    the demon from Hawa-i-ee.

THE DAWN

"You are but children."

Egyptian Priest to Solon.

I

RED of the Dawn !

Screams of a babe in the red-hot palms of a

Moloch of Tyre,

Man with his brotherless dinner on man in the

tropical wood,

Priests in the name of the Lord passing souls

thro' fire to the fire,

Head-hunters and boats of Dahomey that float

upon human blood !

G

II

Red of the Dawn !

Godless fury of peoples, and Christless frolic of kings,

And the bolt of war dashing down upon cities

and blazing farms,

For Babylon was a child new-born, and Rome

was a babe in arms,

And London and Paris and all the rest are as yet

but in leading-strings.

III

Dawn not Day,

While scandal is mouthing a bloodless name

at *her* cannibal feast,

And rake-ruin'd bodies and souls go down in a
common wreck,

And the press of a thousand cities is prized for
it smells of the beast,

Or easily violates virgin Truth for a coin or a
cheque.

IV

Dawn not Day!

Is it Shame, so few should have climb'd from the
dens in the level below,

Men, with a heart and a soul, no slaves of a
four-footed will?

But if twenty million of summers are stored in
the sunlight still,

We are far from the noon of man, there is time
for the race to grow.

V

Red of the Dawn !

Is it turning a fainter red? so be it, but when
shall we lay

The Ghost of the Brute that is walking and
haunting us yet, and be free?

In a hundred, a thousand winters? Ah, what
will *our* children be,

The men of a hundred thousand, a million summers
away?

THE MAKING OF MAN

WHERE is one that, born of woman, altogether can
escape

From the lower world within him, moods of tiger,
or of ape?

Man as yet is being made, and ere the crowning
Age of ages,

Shall not æon after æon pass and touch him into
shape?

All about him shadow still, but, while the races
flower and fade,

Prophet-eyes may catch a glory slowly gaining on

the shade,

Till the peoples all are one, and all their voices

blend in choric

Hallelujah to the Maker 'It is finish'd.   Man is

made.'

THE DREAMER

On a midnight in midwinter when all but the
    winds were dead,
'The meek shall inherit the earth' was a Scripture
    that rang thro' his head,
Till he dream'd that a Voice of the Earth went
    wailingly past him and said :

'I am losing the light of my Youth
  And the Vision that led me of old,
  And I clash with an iron Truth,
  When I make for an Age of gold,
  And I would that my race were run,
  For teeming with liars, and madmen, and
    knaves,

And wearied of Autocrats, Anarchs, and
  Slaves,
And darken'd with doubts of a Faith that
  saves,
And crimson with battles, and hollow with
  graves,
To the wail of my winds, and the moan of
  my waves
I whirl, and I follow the Sun.'

Was it only the wind of the Night shrilling out
  Desolation and wrong
Thro' a dream of the dark ?   Yet he thought that
  he answer'd her wail with a song—

Moaning your losses, O Earth,
  Heart-weary and overdone !

But all's well that ends well,

   Whirl, and follow the Sun !

He is racing from heaven to heaven

   And less will be lost than won,

For all's well that ends well,

   Whirl, and follow the Sun !

The Reign of the Meek upon earth,

   O weary one, has it begun ?

But all's well that ends well,

   Whirl, and follow the Sun !

For moans will have grown sphere-music

   Or ever your race be run !

And all's well that ends well,

   Whirl, and follow the Sun !

MECHANOPHILUS

(In the time of the first railways).

Now first we stand and understand,

And sunder false from true,

And handle boldly with the hand,

And see and shape and do.

Dash back that ocean with a pier,

Strow yonder mountain flat,

A railway there, a tunnel here,

Mix me this Zone with that !

Bring me my horse—my horse ? my wings

That I may soar the sky,

For Thought into the outward springs,

    I find her with the eye.

O will she, moonlike, sway the main,

    And bring or chase the storm,

Who was a shadow in the brain,

    And is a living form ?

Far as the Future vaults her skies,

    From this my vantage ground

To those still-working energies

    I spy nor term nor bound.

As we surpass our fathers' skill,

    Our sons will shame our own ;

A thousand things are hidden still

    And not a hundred known.

And had some prophet spoken true
  Of all we shall achieve,
The wonders were so wildly new
  That no man would believe.

Meanwhile, my brothers, work, and wield
  The forces of to-day,
And plow the Present like a field,
  And garner all you may !

You, what the cultured surface grows,
  Dispense with careful hands :
Deep under deep for ever goes,
  Heaven over heaven expands.

RIFLEMEN FORM!

THERE is a sound of thunder afar,

Storm in the South that darkens the day!

Storm of battle and thunder of war!

Well if it do not roll our way.

Storm, Storm, Riflemen form!

Ready, be ready against the storm!

Riflemen, Riflemen, Riflemen form!

Be not deaf to the sound that warns,

Be not gull'd by a despot's plea!

Are figs of thistles? or grapes of thorns?

How can a despot feel with the Free?

Form, Form, Riflemen Form!

Ready, be ready to meet the storm!

Riflemen, Riflemen, Riflemen form!

Let your reforms for a moment go!

Look to your butts, and take good aims!

Better a rotten borough or so

Than a rotten fleet and a city in flames!

Storm, Storm, Riflemen form!

Ready, be ready against the storm!

Riflemen, Riflemen, Riflemen form!

Form, be ready to do or die!

Form in Freedom's name and the Queen's!

True we have got—*such* a faithful ally

That only the Devil can tell what he means.

Form, Form, Riflemen Form !

Ready, be ready to meet the storm !

Riflemen, Riflemen, Riflemen form ! [1]

---

[1] I have been asked to republish this old poem, which was first published in 'The Times,' May 9, 1859, before the Volunteer movement began.

THE TOURNEY

RALPH would fight in Edith's sight,

    For Ralph was Edith's lover,

Ralph went down like a fire to the fight,

Struck to the left and struck to the right,

    Roll'd them over and over.

'Gallant Sir Ralph,' said the king.

Casques were crack'd and hauberks hack'd,

    Lances snapt in sunder,

Rang the stroke, and sprang the blood,

Knights were thwack'd and riven, and hew'd

    Like broad oaks with thunder.

'O what an arm,' said the king.

Edith bow'd her stately head,

Saw them lie confounded,

Edith Montfort bow'd her head,

Crown'd her knight's, and flush'd as red

As poppies when she crown'd it.

'Take her Sir Ralph,' said the king.

H

THE WANDERER

The gleam of household sunshine ends,

And here no longer can I rest;

Farewell !—You will not speak, my friends,

Unfriendly of your parted guest.

O well for him that finds a friend,

Or makes a friend where'er he come,

And loves the world from end to end,

And wanders on from home to home !

O happy he, and fit to live,

On whom a happy home has power

To make him trust his life, and give

His fealty to the halcyon hour!

I count you kind, I hold you true;

But what may follow who can tell?

Give me a hand—and you—and you—

And deem me grateful, and farewell!

POETS AND CRITICS

This thing, that thing is the rage,

Helter-skelter runs the age ;

Minds on this round earth of ours

Vary like the leaves and flowers,

    Fashion'd after certain laws ;

Sing thou low or loud or sweet,

All at all points thou canst not meet,

    Some will pass and some will pause.

What is true at last will tell :

Few at first will place thee well ;

Some too low would have thee shine,

Some too high—no fault of thine—

   Hold thine own, and work thy will!

Year will graze the heel of year,

But seldom comes the poet here,

   And the Critic's rarer still.

A VOICE SPAKE OUT OF THE SKIES

A VOICE spake out of the skies

To a just man and a wise—

'The world and all within it

Will only last a minute!'

And a beggar began to cry

'Food, food or I die'!

Is it worth his while to eat,

Or mine to give him meat,

If the world and all within it

Were nothing the next minute?

DOUBT AND PRAYER

Tʜᴏ' Sin too oft, when smitten by Thy rod,

Rail at 'Blind Fate' with many a vain

'Alas!'

From sin thro' sorrow into Thee we pass

By that same path our true forefathers trod;

And let not Reason fail me, nor the sod

Draw from my death Thy living flower and

grass,

Before I learn that Love, which is, and was

My Father, and my Brother, and my God!

Steel me with patience ! soften me with grief !

Let blow the trumpet strongly while I pray,

Till this embattled wall of unbelief

My prison, not my fortress, fall away !

Then, if thou willest, let my day be brief,

So Thou wilt strike Thy glory thro' the day.

FAITH

I

DOUBT no longer that the Highest is the wisest
and the best,

Let not all that saddens Nature blight thy hope
or break thy rest,

Quail not at the fiery mountain, at the ship-
wreck, or the rolling

Thunder, or the rending earthquake, or the famine,
or the pest !

11

Neither mourn if human creeds be lower than the

heart's desire !

Thro' the gates that bar the distance comes a gleam

of what is higher.

Wait till Death has flung them open, when the

man will make the Maker

Dark no more with human hatreds in the glare of

deathless fire !

THE SILENT VOICES

WHEN the dumb Hour, clothed in black,

Brings the Dreams about my bed,

Call me not so often back,

Silent Voices of the dead,

Toward the lowland ways behind me,

And the sunlight that is gone !

Call me rather, silent voices,

Forward to the starry track

Glimmering up the heights beyond me

On, and always on !

GOD AND THE UNIVERSE

I

WILL my tiny spark of being wholly vanish in your

deeps and heights?

Must my day be dark by reason, O ye Heavens,

of your boundless nights,

Rush of Suns, and roll of systems, and your fiery

clash of meteorites?

II

'Spirit, nearing yon dark portal at the limit of thy

human state,

Fear not thou the hidden purpose of that Power
which alone is great,

Nor the myriad world, His shadow, nor the silent
Opener of the Gate.'

THE DEATH

OF THE

DUKE OF CLARENCE AND AVONDALE

To the Mourners

THE bridal garland falls upon the bier,

The shadow of a crown, that o'er him hung,

Has vanish'd in the shadow cast by Death.

So princely, tender, truthful, reverent, pure —

Mourn! That a world-wide Empire mourns with

you,

That all the Thrones are clouded by your loss,

Were slender solace.   Yet be comforted ;

For if this earth be ruled by Perfect Love,

Then, after his brief range of blameless days,

The toll of funeral in an Angel ear

Sounds happier than the merriest marriage-bell.

The face of Death is toward the Sun of Life,

His shadow darkens earth : his truer name

Is 'Onward,' no discordance in the roll

And march of that Eternal Harmony

Whereto the worlds beat time, tho' faintly heard

Until the great Hereafter.   Mourn in hope !

THE END

Printed by R. & R. CLARK, *Edinburgh.*

www.ingramcontent.com/pod-product-compliance
Lightning Source LLC
Chambersburg PA
CBHW030537270326
41927CB00008B/1421